Survival Prepping

Hunting, Fishing, Foraging, Trapping and Eating Insects

Survival Guide Box Set:
3 Books In 1

By Rick Canton

Book 1

Survival Guide

Foraging Edible Plants

How to Survive by Foraging for Edible Plants

TABLE OF CONTENTS

INTRODUCTION

Whether you're a weekend camper, or prepping for the apocalypse, knowing which plants can sustain your body is a valuable tool to have in your information arsenal.

Survival Guide Foraging Edible Plants - How to Survive by Foraging For Edible Plants was written to educate those interested in learning how to live off of the land by foraging, and as a resource to use if you find yourself in an emergency situation without a reliable food source. Our hunting and gathering ancestors ate these plants as they roamed across the plains, but over time we've lost these basic skills.

Note: Please see the link at the end of this book to view all of the pictures in high resolution. For those of you reading on a Kindle paperwhite, the images in this book might be difficult to see. I've created a post with full-scale images and linked it in the conclusion.

CHAPTER 1

AmaranthusRetroflexus

Location of plant

AmaranthusRetroflexus, generally known as Amaranthus, is a plant common to the North American continent. It can be seen from Canada to the U.S., and Mexico,and also along both the Atlantic and Pacific coasts. This plant growswild on other continents, such as: Europe, Eurasia, Africa and South America. In the U.S, this plant is seen in places like the Colorado Plateau, the Upper Missouri Basin & Broken Lands, Cascades Mountains, Rocky Mountain Piedmont, Sierra Mountains, the Colombia Plateau, and also the Wyoming Basin. Other locations are the Northern Pacific Border, Southern Pacific Border, Upper Basin & Range, Lower Basin & Range, Northern and Middle Rocky Mountains, Southern Rocky Mountains, Great Plains, and Black Hills Uplift.

Information about plant

AmaranthusRetroflexus (scientific name) is nicknamed as 'male finger.' It is also commonly known as redroot pigweed, common amaranth and green amaranth. This edible plant can grow up to three to six feet tall. It has pinnate raised underside of every leaf. Its leaves are ovate to elliptic in shape and its branches grow occasionally. The growth of the leaves is seasonal—spring into summer, while it seeds during summer or fall. It can grow in both poor and rich soil for as long as there is moisture and sunlight available. There is no record of hazardous effects from this plant. Greeks used to consider Amaranthusas a sacred plant because of its healing properties. As such, it became a symbol of immortality. The Greeks also used its branches to adorn the images of their deities and memorial tombs. The Aztecs have used this plant in a number of ways. Amaranthus became one of the ingredients of their religious foods, through Amaranth flour mixed with human blood, thus making dough. In other cultures, the seeds have been used to make confections, gruel (oatmeal-like food) and even beer. Etymologically, 'amaranth' originated from the Greek language, which means 'unfading.'

How to eat plant

This edible weed can be eaten in the raw as a whole. Just take careful notice of the spines that are present on the leaves. These may cause infection ifingested. Although not poisonous by nature, its leaves may contain oxalic acid and nitrates, which are sipped from soil that has high content of nitrates. Boiling the leaves is a good way to remove these chemicals, but you should not consume the boiled water. The seeds, leaves and flowers of this plant are great sources of vitamins and minerals. The Amaranth seeds contain high protein, amino acids and fibre. It also has vitamins such as A, C, and E and minerals like calcium, iron, potassium and phosphorus. Ripeness is determined by gently shaking or rubbing the flower spike. If it readily falls from the flower spike, the plant and its seeds are ripe and can be harvested. You can collect the seeds from the

Amaranth by gently side-tipping the plant, then rubbing or shaking the spikes over a container, allowing the seeds to collect there. All the parts can be crushed and used together and can be a great remedy against stomachache due to acid, or to treat insect & snakebites and wounds.

CHAPTER 2:

Cattail (TyphaLatifolia)

Location of plant

Cattails are scientifically and generally known as Typha. Common cattails are more specifically called TyphaLatifolia. This wild plant often grows in places surrounded by trees and usually in communities that are favourable with moist climates or open water. It also dominantly grows in locations with frequent flood occurrences. Cattails can be found in Australia, Africa, the UK, India, Eurasia and North America. In the United States, it grows throughout all the states with the exception of Hawaii and the U.S. territory of Puerto Rico. TyphaLatifolia is common to climates that are tropical and subtropical. Other climates where it can survive are humid coastal, dry continental, southern and northern temperature.

Information about plant

TyphaLatifolia is a plant-species that has flowers which resemble a cat's tail, thus its common name (cattail.) This plant grows very quickly and reaches heights up to nine feet tall. It has densely packed, tiny flowers consisting of male flowers along the top cluster, and female flowers at the lower portion of the cluster. Because of these properties, it is classified as monoecious, where both male and female flowers are on the same plant. Its flowers become brown in color when at its full bloom. Its yellow-green stem can grow more than a foot long. The typha leaves are shaped like long grasses, which are thick and grayish-green. Furthermore, cattails have very small, numerous seeds. This plant blooms during mid to late summer. Because of the flowers unique form, some use it for playing and others utilize it for floral arrangement. Nevertheless, this flowering plant can be a native to any pond or place for as long as the presence of water is there. As far as written history is concerned, cattails were used as a food source during the 17th century and even further in the past. Cattails have been found in caves dating back to the 8th century. Ancient civilizations,such as the Chinese and Egyptian used to consider this wild plant as a prized food. It is a food rich in fiber. Native tribes from North America also used to consider cattails as a precious source of food, which provided starch for bread making. History tells us that this plant was also used in religious ceremonies as well.

How to eat plant

Cattails have always been an important source of food in wild life. In fact, Euell Gibbons noted this idea by saying, "For the number of different kinds of food it produces, there is no plant, wild or domesticated, which tops the common cattail." This species of plant has no record of toxic substance, which made it a staple food during ancient times. At present, it is still edible; just make sure that the area where it is taken from is pollution-free. The rootstocks are absolutely edible as well as its young shoots, in which two can be eaten raw. The mud must be removed. The pre-bloomed spikes of the flowers can be eaten after boiling. When cooked, cattails have the same flavour as corn. The spikes can also be eaten raw.

CHAPTER 3:

Chicory (CichoriumIntybus)

Location of plant

Chicory, with the scientific name of, *CichoriumIntybus*, is an edible plant species, which originated in the Mediterranean region and was known as a green salad when distributed to many parts of the world. It became popular in North America during the 18th century, and by 1950 it became one of the import products of the continent for economical purpose. It is popular in southern Canada and the United States where it has naturally grown. Because of this, this plant reproduces abundantly along roadsides and highways. It is common in the state of Ohio. Although cultivated, Chicory can be found naturally in open fields like lawns, pastures and wastelands. This plant thrives best in soils rich in lime butit can survive in various types of soil.

Information about plant

The word 'Intybus' is an Egyptian term for the month of January, the month when Chicory were harvested and eaten long ago in ancient Egypt. At present, Chicory flowers bloom from June until September. Their blossoms open in the morning and close when the sunlight is at its brightest. The plant produces an average of 3000 seeds. Initially, the plant grows with irregular leaves, which later shed, leaving behind a leafless stem tipped with its flowers. This plant reproduces using its seeds. Cultivation is not tolerated on this plant.

How to eat plant

Chicory is a good food source because it is easily digested. All parts of the plant are edible—the flowers, leaves and roots. You may harvest the young leaves and eat them raw or boil them. The leaves have an innate bitterness in taste, which can be lessened by cooking in water. The roots are delicious when boiled; howeverthe roots can be eaten right away if cooking isn't convenient or hunger is immanent. Chicory can be used as seasoning for foods through drying and grinding the roots. When roasted and pulverize, the Chicory roots can be a good substitute or additive for coffee. The flowers can be eaten like quick and satisfying snacks. The good thing about this plant is that it has a property called 'tannis' that can help during digestion and can reduce intestinal parasites making Chicory an important addition to your diet when living off the land.

CHAPTER 4:

Dandelion (Taraxacumofficinale)

Location of plant

Dandelion is one of the most common weeds scattered across the continents of Asia, Europe and North America. Scientifically known as Taraxacumofficinale, dandelions originally grew on French sub-Antarctic islands. The weed then spread to many regions of the worldduring a time when the presence of animals, like rabbits, and climate warming caused the death of essential plants in various areas. Dandelions then became more widespread. This plant is also found in Africa, South America and Australia. It is also located in all fiftyU.S. states and in most provinces of Canada. This plant is considered as a noxious weed in other territories because of the major damage it wrought to the agricultural industry worldwide. The Dandelion's ability to reproduce faster (an estimation of production of almost one hundred million seeds per hectare) causes quite a headache to major crops. Seeds can be transported easily through wind and can spread hundreds of meters from the source. Moreover, this weed can adapt to almost any type of soil and the seeds are not dependent to cold temperatures as long as it is in considerable part of the soil. Dandelion growth occurs in areas like agricultural lands, coastlands, and grasslands and even in urban areas.

Information about plant

Dandelion sprouts from the unbranched taproots. It can produce anywhere from one to more than ten stems and has a typical height of five to forty cm. Some may grow as much asseventy cm tall (twototwenty-seven inches.) Its stems are usually upright and lax with a purplish color. It can produce flower heads that are taller than the foliage or the leaves of the plants. The leaves may grow upright but they can spread horizontally. The petioles that support the leaves have either narrow wings or remain unwinged. There are times that the stems have shorts hairs, while others are glabrous. The dandelion leaves can resemble a fish skeleton and have an average length of five to forty-five cm (twototen inches) and a width of one to ten cm (one-halftotwo inches.) The term 'dandelion' derives from the French words "dent de lion" which means lion's tooth, referring to the coarsely-toothed leaves of the plant. When this plant flowers, the blossom's color is yellow. When it is about to bring out seeds, the yellow petals and the leaves underneath close and the plant forms a 'head' that will produce the seeds. The blossomed head is white like a puffball. Some cultures consider dandelions as the only plant that represents the sun, the moon and the stars. The yellow flowers represent the sun. The puffball is for the moon and the seeds are the stars.

How to eat plant

Dandelions are edible and can be harvested anywhere the wild. On a small scale, they are cultivated as a leaf vegetable. The leaves can be eaten raw or they can also be cooked. It can be an ingredient to add flavour to soups or salads. Young leaves and buds that are unopened are usually also eaten raw and the mature leaves are cooked or boiled to remove the bitter taste.Dandelion 'greens' are sometimes a substitute to collard greens in the Southern United States. Dandelion has slight bitter taste. The roots and the flowers are also edible. The roots can be steeped in boiling water and the water from that can be sipped like ahot tea. Dandelion is rich in vitamins A and C, and minerals like iron and calcium. It has higher levels of iron and calcium than spinach.

CHAPTER 5:

Lamb's Quarter (Chenopodium album)

Location of plant

Chenopodium album is an edible plant that can be found in most parts of Europe. This plant species is also found in the Asian region, although it differs in specimen structure with the European species. It has been introduced already to Africa, Australasia, Oceania and North America. It is present in Canada and in every state of the United States. Chenopodium album, also known as "Lamb's quarter," can grow in any place with soils that are nitrogen-rich.

Information about plant

Lamb's Quarter can grow to over a meter in height, but it begins to bend after flowering due to the weight of the seeds and foliage. Its leaves are arranged alternatively and can have a variety of appearances depending upon the leaves' position from the plant's base. The leaves near the base are toothed and have a diamond shape, which are three to seven cm long and three to six cm in width (one to two inches.) Leaves on the upper portion are full and lanceolate-rhomboid in shape, having a length of one to five cm (one inch) and 0.4 to two cm width and are waxy in appearance. The flowers can grow up to ten to forty cm (three to fifteen inches) in length.

In the Flora of North America, Clemants and Mosyakin considered Chenopodium album as "one of the worst weeds and most widespread synanthropic plants on the Earth." Synanthropic means 'human-associated.'This plant is considered 'one of the worst weeds' because of its rapid reproduction, which depends upon the condition of the environment. Chenopodium album can reproduce certain amounts of seeds. In optimal conditions, it may produce thousands of seeds. This activity can greatly affect the reproduction of any nearby crops.

Historically, Vikings and Romans used to mix the seeds with their grains and also storage areas and ovens in their ancient territories. In India, this plant is abundant during winter season and is used in popular dishes such as soups, curries and breads. Other cultures use the seeds to brew alcoholic beverages.

How to eat plant

Lamb's quarter is very safe to eat, in particularly, its leaves can be eaten in the raw or cooked like spinach. Although edible, the leaves should be taken in moderation because of the presence of oxalic acid, which is an acid helpful in breaking down calcium. It is not safe to consume when not taken to serve a purpose. Like other plants that grow wild, nitrogen content in the soil should always be a caution,as it may be present in the plant. Lamb's quarter leaves can be boiled or wilted if preferred. The young leaves are best to eat. The black seeds of the lamb's quarter provide a very good source of protein, Vitamin A, calcium, phosphorus and also potassium.

Others have suggested that the seeds are better when soaked overnight to remove the saponins (a toxic substance) from the surface. They can also be boiled and crushed or ground to a paste. The seeds can be an added ingredient to flour mixtures for breads or to soups and beverages for texture and flavour.

CHAPTER 6:

Miner's Lettuce (ClatoniaPerfoliata)

Location of plant

Miner's lettuce, scientifically known as,ClatoniaPerfoliata, is an annual plant found and grown naturally in North America's western mountains and coastal areas. It grows from the U.S. territory of Alaska and throughout Canada's British Columbia, down to the Central America region. It is also native to the state of California, specifically the areas surrounding Sacramento, California as well as thenorthern regions of San Joaquin valleys. Other sub-species of this plant are found in Arizona and Utah and parts of Mexico, down to Guatemala in Central America. Miner's Lettuce is a seasonal plant that sprouts during spring due to its favourable adaptation to cooler climates. It usually appears after the first heavy rains of the spring. Miner's lettuce is found under the shades of taller trees, such as fir, pine and oak trees. It can also be found in fields that grow wheatgrass and bluegrass. During summer seasons, the leaves of this plant dry out, turning red in color, which is a natural reaction to many plant species that are accustomed to cold weather.

Information about plant

Miner's lettuce grows in the wild. Its leaves are usually rosette-formingwith small flowers which can be found at the center of a lettuce's leaf. The seed leaf of this plant is commonly light green, though sometimes purplish or brownish-green. It is also thick, long and narrow in shape. It can grow maturely at minimum of one cm and maximum of forty cm (less than an inch, up to fifteen inches.) The first real leaves sprout from the rosette of the plant's base and these can expand up to one-half to four cm (one inch) in length. The long petiole of the lettuce can have a length of up to twenty cm (eight inches.) Flowers are at the tip of a short stem and are usually white or pink in color. The petals are usually two to six mm long, appearing seasonally before summer or in early summer (February to May or June.)

How to eat plant

This plant has crunchy leaves with a mild, sweet flavour. The flowers are also tender. Although considered by many as weed, this plant is highly edible and in fact, it is loaded with vitamins needed to sustain the body. During the period of the famous Gold Rush, miners used to eat this plant to prevent scurvy (a disease caused by very low Vitamin C in the body and can cause bleeding of skin and loosening of teeth and spongy gums.) The miners made this plant a staple of their survival food stores,which later gave ClatoniaPerfoliataits more common name. The native Indians of California taught the miners this diet technique. This plant can actually be eaten raw, such as an additive to a fresh salad or boiled like spinach. Miner's lettuce contains high essential vitamins like beta carotene (found in carrots,) Vitamin C as well as protein. According to a study by the Journal of the American Dietetic Association, a hundred grams of miner's lettuce contains one-third of a persons' Vitamin C daily requirements, and twenty-two percent of the Vitamin A requirements. It also contains iron (ten percent of the daily requirement.) It is a very good food source to revive a person's system after a long winter's diet of heavy meats and dried grains.

CHAPTER 7:

Prickly Pear Cactus (Opuntia)

Location of plant

The Prickly Pear cactus is a plant which grows in Africa, Australia, South America and North America, mostly in desert areas that are not rich in water sources. In the U.S., Prickly Pear cactus can be found in all of the deserts in south-western America, grown in different species and different elevations. Just like the other cacti, this plant grows in dry soil and rock and well-drained slopes. Others can be found in juniper forests or forests which have evergreen trees,while some grow in high rocky slopes on mountain foothills.

Information about plant

The Prickly Pear's scientific name is Opuntia. This plant can adapt to a wide range of temperatures and almost any amount or absence of moisture. Just like the other cacti, it flourishes best in sunny and desert-like areas. It is characterized by oval shaped pads that resemble large leaves. These pads are flat, fleshy and green in colour. The pads store water for the cactus and usually grow to ten to forty-six cm in length (four to eighteen inches.) They have a width of twenty-three cm (nine inches) or more. The cactus can grow from one to seven feet tall or 2.1 m. The pads of this plant have long sharp spines. The other spines, which are harder to see, are called glochids. Glochids appear to be harmless but once inside a person's skin, they are difficult to remove and can cause skin irritations that last up to several days. The Prickly Pear cactus grows and bears fruits from early spring up until summer. Fruits blossom at the edges of the pads and are covered in hairy-like thorns which must be dealt with carefully. They are usually purple in color in the U.S. and are cylindrical in shape with an average of seven cm (three inches) in length. Other places like Mexico, the Prickly Pear bears white fruits. The fruits ripen until late fall but the months from September to November are the best time for the ripened fruits. These fruits can last for a week when stored after harvesting. Harvesting of fruits must be done very carefully as the tiny thorns might look innocent but can feel like the prick of dozens of pins when touched by bare hands.

How to eat plant

The pads and fruits of this kind of cactus are highly edible. Once harvested, the fruits can be carefully peeled and eaten raw. They can be dried or you can extract juice from the inside. Indications that the fruits have ripened are when the outer layer is bright red and the inside flesh has turned orange. Some processed foods use the flesh of the cactus as syrups and jellies. In other circumstances, it is fermented to produce a liquor. The flesh is also an effective water purifier, according to the researches at the University of South Florida. When extracting the pads and the glochids, it should be noted that tools such as a knife, fork and gloves should be used when removing them from the soil and when removing the spikes. Any survival knife should do the trick, but when tongs are available these are best for harvesting the fruits. Caution: the spikes of the pads are very painful when lodged in the skin. The young stem of the plant can be eaten raw, yet it is best when boiled first. The cactus is very tasty and has much nutritional value. No doubt, this is by far the best survival food source when stranded in a desert climate.

CHAPTER 8:

Purslane (Portulacaoleracea)

Location of plant

Purslane can be found in most parts of the North American continent, and throughout the Middle East, Indian region, and Oceania. It reached North America before Christopher Columbus. Evidence of Purslane was found in the Crawford Lake during the 15th century. It is widely known today as an exotic weed, although in other places this plant is naturalized. It can grow in many parts of the world and can adapt to tropical and temperate conditions. It is common in most Asian regions as well. It is also usually found in waste areas, roadsides and agricultural fields.

Information about plant

Purslane is scientifically known as *Portulacaoleracea*. Its more common nickname is pigweed. This plant has thick leaves and usually grows low to the ground. It also grows extremely fast and has the ability produce leaves that are highly edible. Due to its fast propagation, from the quick seed production and its survivability in any type of soil, many considered it as a weed, while others think of it as a vegetable. It is characterized by purplish-red stems where leaves grow in an alternate sequence. Flowers may appear occasionally and are yellow in color. These flowers are usually six mm wide. Purslane seeds are tiny and black and the root is composed of fibrous root that is able to survive in poor soil, requiring less water. Centuries ago it was used as a food source as well as medicine. The word Protulaca is a Latin term portula, which means "gate," referring to the covering of the seed capsule. Oleracea means "kitchen vegetable." In Spain, it is known as "verdolaga" and in France, it is called "poupier." Purslane can be used as first aid for burns. In other cultures, they fry purslane, and sometimes mix it with soups and stews as a thickening agent. It is frequently featured in Turkish, Persian and Lebanese dishes.

How to eat plant

Although many have considered purslane as weed, it has an abundance of vitamins and minerals that is not often found in just one food. It contains many omega-3 fatty acids that can help the brain and heart. It also contains vitamins A, C and minerals like calcium, iron, magnesium and potassium. It also has antioxidant properties. Purslane has a sour taste and has a mucilaginous quality or slightly sticky. The leaves, stems, flowers and seeds are very edible. They can be eaten raw. They can also be boiled before consumption to remove the sour taste. The Purslane leaf is considered a leaf vegetable. Mahatma Gandhi, a famous Indian leader, considered this among his favourite foods. In any survival situation this is a great food source to help maintain energy.

CHAPTER 9:

Shepherd's-Purse (Capsella bursa-pastoris)

Location of plant

Shepherd's-purse is a floweringplant, which is native in the eastern part of Europe and the nearby Asia Minor. It is one of the most wellknown and common weeds in the world. It grows in colder climates, but it is not native to some regions like China and North America, where climates are cooler. It is considered an archaeophyte plant to those places, which basically means it is grown and transported from one territory to another. It is also archaeophyte in North Africa and in the Mediterranean region as well. Shepherd's Purse grows annually in the winter season and can sprout in coastal areas that have cooler temperatures, such as the state of California. It may also grow in agricultural lands, and along roadsides.

Information about plant

Capsella bursa-pastoris is the scientific name of Shepherd's-purse. It is called that because of its triangular shape and purse-like pods. It is also known as case weed, mother's heart, and witches'-pouches. This plant species is part of the mustard family. Shepherd's-purse initially blooms during spring season. This plant can grow to about fifty cm (twenty inches) tall. Its leaves have a variety of shapes and are covered with small hair like fibres. The cluster of leaves can be three to ten cm (four inches) long. The stems grow at the center of the rosette leaves and are usually thin and green in color. The flower blossoms grow at the tips of the stems. Its color is white and has four petals. The flowers are at first clustered but as time passes, the stalks lengthen and create pods for the seeds. Every pod has one to two brown oval-shaped seeds. This plant reproduces only through its seeds. Depending on the temperature and the environment, Shepherd's-purse can produce between 500 to 90,000 seeds. They are then dispersed naturally by the wind and rain as well as by animal and human activities. The seeds of Shepherd's-purse are used as an ingredient for poultry feeds, which aids in the production of quality of eggs.

How to eat plant

The best motivation to eat this plant is the nutritional value it contains. Shepherd's-purse provides a high amount of vitamin C, calcium, and iron. It is also a good source of carbohydrates and proteins. Acetylcholine is also present in Shepherd's-purse, which is helpful for the nervous system. This plant has a peppery flavourwith a pungent odour. The plant can be eaten raw, or if preferred as a cooked potherb. It can also be a good seasoning to provide flavour to any food. It should be cautioned that its leaves and seeds are made up of glucosinolates that can cause digestive irritation. This can be avoided through moderate consumption. It is an ideal survival plant for hikers and campers whenever foods have run out.

CHAPTER 10:

Wild Onions/Garlics (Allium canadense)

Location of plant

Allium Canadense is native plant found in the eastern part of North America. This plant was naturalized in Cuba. Also known as Wild Garlic or Wild Onion, it can be found in the New England territories of the U.S.such as Maine, New Hampshire, Rhode Island, Connecticut, Massachusetts and Vermont. Other regions use this plant species for decorations and herbs for culinary purposes. Its natural habitats are floodplains and forests.

Information about plant

This plant has an edible bulb with a brown fibre covering on its skin. It has a taste and smell similar to an onion. Another type of this plant (crow garlic) possesses a stronger garlic taste. Wild Onions are characterized with narrow leaves, resembling blades of grass extending from its stem and topped by star-shaped cluster of flowers. Flowers can be either pink or white. Occasionally, bulbletswill replace the flowers partially or as a whole.When this happens, the flowers become hermaphroditic, having both male and female properties. This plant flowers during spring and early summer (May to June.)

Allium is the Latin term for onion. In the Celtic language, this originated from the word 'all,' which means pungent. The Celtic word 'Alla,' denotes feirie. Canadense is from the country name of Canada, which may convey also North America generally.

Wild Onions can be dangerous to animals like cattle when consumed in large amounts, while lesser doses of it can improve milk's flavour. In other cultures, they use Wild Onion as an insect-repellent.

How to eat plant

The smell of wild onions and garlics can determine its edibility. For example if the aroma is similar to an onion or garlic, it can be eaten. When you don't smell either of the two, it is an acknowledgement that it isn't quite ripe enough for consumption. Even worse, at this stage it could be toxic. There are some plants in Florida that look like this, but have no aroma. These are also considered toxic. When ripe, all parts of this plant can be eaten—the bulbs underground, the leaves, the blossoms and bulblets as well. The small cloves in the plant where it flowers are the bulblets. Thesebulblets are easy to harvest. The underground bulbs are also easy to harvest and can be found just four to six inches beneath the soil. Although it's commonly known as 'onion,' it is also called 'garlic,' primarily because of its garlic-like aroma. This plant is generally mild in taste and can add much flavour to a variety of soups and stews.

CONCLUSION

There are many types of edible plants in North America. It's important to learn which ones are edible, their nutritional value, and how they can be foraged and prepared for consumption. A human can live on plants alone and if you're ever in a situation where foraging is your only option, you'll be grateful that you educated yourself.

If you found this guide helpful, or would like to add a plant we might have missed, please leave us a comment on the review page.

Book 2

Survival Guide

Eating Insects

How to Survive by Eating Insects and Learning Entomophagy

TABLE OF CONTENTS

INTRODUCTION

This book was written for anyone who has an interest or curiosity in Entomophagy, which is the practice of consuming insects as a food source. The eggs, larvae, pupae and adults of certain insect species have been eaten by humans since ancient times and can be an excellent source of nutrition even in modern times.

Human insect consumption hasalmost always been common to cultures across most parts of the world, including North, Central and South America, Africa, Asia, Australia and New Zealand. Over 1,000 species of insects are known to be safe for humans to eat. There are around 3,000 ethnic groups who are known to practiceEntomophagy. However, in some societies insect-eating is seen as taboo and is rare in the Western world, but insects remain a popular food in many developing regions of Latin America, Africa, Asia and Oceania.

From the diehard survivalists to the average camper who wants to be prepared if something happens to their food supplies while out in the wild, this book is an invaluable resource.

As you'll learn, insects are great source of nutrition, and can sustain a human indefinitely. It is my goal to educate you on which insects can provide the best nutrients for your body.

CHAPTER 1:

Short-Horned Grasshopper

Insect Info:

Entomophagy is the human practice of eating insects and covers a vast range of animal species, from moth, beetle, and bee larvae, to cockroaches and crickets. Many insects provide important nutritional value for those with limited food supplies in the wild, or even as part of a regular daily diet. Insects are not only plentiful, but most of them are safe to eat and provide essential sources of protein, sugars, fats, vitamins, and minerals. This e-book describes ten edible insects that can be found across the U.S, including where to find them and how to prepare them for consumption.

The first on our list of edible insects is the grasshopper. Like locusts and crickets, grasshoppers are abundant throughout

North America and are easily prepared for eating. Grasshoppers are also known as short-horned grasshoppers, a name which helps distinguish them from the other insect species of the *Orthoptera* family. Other members of this family include *katydids*, or bush crickets, and locusts, which refer to grasshoppers when they change color and swarm in large groups. Many crickets and locusts are also edible.

Grasshoppers inhabit meadows, hedgerows, fields, and forests. Because they often use camouflage, either to hide from or startle prey, they can be difficult to spot. However, grasshoppers are easily found by the chirping sound the males make when rubbing their hind legs against their forewings. Once you've located an appropriate site, a simple trap can be constructed quickly and easily using a Mason jar and some bait. Dig a small hole in the ground in the site, place the jar into the hole, and cover the outside of the jar with soil. Then place some fruit or plant matter, such as apple, carrot, or lettuce, inside the jar and wait until the following day before checking the trap. You can also add water to the jar to drown any grasshoppers that find their way inside. If there are several people in your group, and you are in need of large quantities, you can collect grasshoppers by walking in a connected line through long grass, effectively herding the insects into a trap.

In Uganda, grasshoppers are collected on a mass scale using large angled sheets of galvanized tin roofing placed inside standing oil drums. At night time, powerful electric light is directed onto the tin sheets. Grasshoppers are drawn to the reflected light and slide down into the oil drums where they are trapped in massive quantities.

In North America, the grasshopper is a less common food source, though survival experts and outdoor enthusiasts have relied on this insect to provide vital protein and calcium. There are numerous species in the U.S., including the lubber grasshopper, which has red wings lined with black and can measure two to 2.8 inches. The smaller and more imaginatively named,'cattail toothpick' grasshopper has transparent wings, and is found in large numbers in the southern United States.

How To Eat:

When fried, the Nsenene grasshopper of Uganda is said to resemble chicken or shrimp in flavour. Grasshoppers are a delicacy in many other parts of the world too. In Mexico, for example, people eat grasshoppers, or *chapulines*, roasted with chili and lime. In Japan, they are known as *inago* when they are candied and enjoyed as a cocktail snack. Whatever their preparation, grasshoppers make a crunchy and enjoyable treat, and can form part of a staple diet when foraging in the wild.

Short-horned grasshoppers range in size from 0.2 to 4.3 inches in length and many species are green or light brown, which enable them to camouflage themselves in the undergrowth. Per 3.5 ounce serving, raw grasshoppers provide from one-half to one ounce of protein depending on the species. This serving provides twenty-five to sixty percent of the protein needed daily for a healthy diet. They also contain unsaturated fats, iron and calcium.

It's best to cook grasshoppers for at least a few minutes to make them safe to eat. You can boil, fry, or roast grasshoppers, adding different spices and seasonings as you see fit. Many people enjoy them roasted with salt and oil. It is recommended to remove the legs and wings before eating since they might irritate your throat and provide and unpleasant texture. Grasshoppers can also be dried and stored for future use, especially if you have other food sources available to you.

CHAPTER 2:

Honeypot Ant

Insect Info:

Next on the list of edible insects is the honeypot ant. This species of ant has specialized worker ants (*repletes*) that are gorged on food causing their abdomens to swell, which then provides nutrition to the other ants in times of famine. When needed, other ants will extract nourishment from these repletes. Honeypot ants are therefore a kind of living larder for their colonies, though they can also provide a sweet treat for people in desert regions across the globe.

The abdomen of the replete is swollen with a nectar-like fluid that can become so large that the ants are often unable to leave the nest. (A replete can increase its body weight up to eight times.) During wetter weather, other worker ants begin feeding repletes to fatten them up for use in drier weather when food is scarce. Mostly, the repletes are fed nectar and other sugary plant fluids, as well as aphid honeydew and small insects. Often, competing colonies invade one another with the victor taking control of the other's nest and food supply, including the engorged repletes.

Several species are found in western parts of the U.S, as well as in New Mexico, Arizona, and arid and semi-arid regions, particularly on the edges of desert and sometimes in dry woodland. More recently in America, people have been known to farm honeypot ants for human consumption. Honeypot ants can be identified in various colors, including green and blue, as well as in different sizes. Often, they are dark red in color and measure one-quarter inch to one-half inch in length. They can always be identified by their abdominal swellings.

How To Eat:

Honeypot ants have been eaten by humans in various desert regions for many years. In the Australian Outback, aboriginal people have been known to eat honeypot ants as a delicacy. Finding water-based sustenance when living in or moving through desert areas can be especially difficult for ants and humans alike, so honeypot ants provide a welcome and refreshing treat.

In the case of the aboriginal people of the Australian Outback, *Camponotusinflatus*, a type of honeypot ant, are dug up from the ground and eaten raw. Honeypot ants live for most of their lives underground and must therefore be dug up. You might have to dig three to five feet down though, and you will have to contend with agitating the other ants as you dig.

The taste of a honeypot ant is determined by what it has been fed and can vary in sweetness. Typically, honeypot ants are made up of natural sugars and water, which of course are vital resources in the wild.

CHAPTER 3:

Formosan Termite

Insect Info:

The termite is in the same family as the cockroach and makes a reliable and plentiful food source. The Formosan termite is a subterranean termite which ischaracterized by large populations that share interconnected foraging galleries in soil.This species of termite is considered a pest and is widely distributed across the U.S. Most often, termites feed on dead plant material, typically wood, leaf litter, soil, or animal excreta. They also eat bone and decaying animal matter, and traces of termites have even been found on dinosaur bones.

Termites are more abundant in subtropical and tropical regions where humidity is high, though they can also be found in drier climates. The diversity of the termite species is low in North America, though a large number of colonies belonging to over fifty species have been identified across the continent.

Most termite nests are found underground, or in fallen trees and neglected timber, though some are built inside living trees or as huge mounds. Digging up a Formosan termite nest can yield a great deal of food, though agitated termites might cause you some irritation. Note that although Formosan termites have the capability to bite humans, they much prefer chewing wood and it is unlikely that you will get bitten.

Most often, termites are white or yellow in color, though they can sometimes be dark red, brown, or black.

How To Eat:

Termites are consumed in many different places around the world. In parts of Africa, termites, or *alates*, are an important part of the diet, which also includes worker and queen ants. However, queen antsare regarded as a delicacy since they are more difficult to locate. Alates are collected at the onset of the rainy season, often close to sources of electric light, to which termites are attracted. Usually, termites are eaten when crops are undeveloped and when livestock is lean. Termites are also enjoyed in Thailand and are known as *Maeng Mao*. Consumption has been limited to indigenous populations of Asia and North and South America, though in recent years they have become increasingly valued as a food source throughout the U.S.

Termites contain all of the essential amino acids needed by humans as suggested by the World Health Organization. Typically, their wings are removed before roasting slowly on a hot plate or dry-fried in a pan until crisp. Some people eat them with a little salt, though you do not need to add oil during cooking since termites contain oil. Termites can measure 0.16-0.59 inches and contain adequate levels of fat and protein. Per 3.5 ounce serving, termites have one-half ounce of protein and contain five percent calcium. For this serving, termites deliver over six hundred calories, which can provide substantial energy to your body when food is scarce.

The largest termite known, *Macrotermesbellicosus*, has been found to be rich in vitamins A and C, with varying protein and vitamin levels in worker ants and queens. Worker ants are higher in protein and vitamin C while queens are higher in vitamin A. Certain species of termites in forested areas are said to taste like minty wood, while others have a nuttier flavour.

CHAPTER 4:

June Bug

Insect Info:

The June bug is a genus of beetle in the *Scarabaeidae* family. They take their name from the month in which they emerge as adults and begin to swarm. They are a common species of beetle and can be found across the globe, not only in remote areas but also in large cities.

June bugs are found throughout North America. The green June bug is found in southeastern U.S., the ten-lined June bug inhabits western U.S and Canada, the figeater June bug lives in the western and southwestern U.S. And the European chafer, which is native to continental Europe, has now alsospread to the U.S.

Typically, June bugs are found on plants or near lights.They are blackish or reddish-brown in colour, but do not often have prominent markings. They also have rather hairy legs. These beetles are nocturnal, but they are drawn to light in great numbers. Their wings are stored beneath a hard shell and when held, a June bug often makes a huffing sound by rubbing its abdomen against its shell. Adult June bugs swarm in large numbers on summer evenings and many species are attracted to bright sources of light. Because of this, a good method for collecting June bugs is to shine a powerful flashlight onto a white bed sheet at night. As they gather along the sheet, you can scoop them into a jar. You can also search for them on or under plants during the evening while they are feeding. June bugs can be caught easily since they are often clumsy in their movements, and sometimes not moving at all.

How To Eat:

Native Americans have enjoyed June bugs by roasting them on hot coals, though they can be grilled or fried as well. June bugs are a good insect for beginnerEntomophagiststo collect because there are no other similar looking insects that are toxic to confuse with the June bug. Typically, they are less than one inch in length and can be eaten either as a larva or as an adult. The larvae, or white grubs, feed on grass roots or other herbs. The grubs are whitish with a brownish-black head with conspicuous brown spiracles along the sides of its body.Whether larva or adult, June bugs are easy to locate and can be prepared quickly before eating. The taste of a June bug has often been described as buttery or resembling that of a walnut. It's a good idea to remove the legs and wings before eating to avoid an unpleasant crunch. For a 3.5 ounce serving, June bugs provide nearly one-half ounce of protein, small amounts of fat and carbohydrates, with trace amounts of calcium and iron.

CHAPTER 5:

Eastern Tent Caterpillar

Insect Info:

All caterpillars are the larvae of moths or butterflies, and many of them are fit for human consumption. The eastern tent caterpillar is among twenty-six identified species of tent caterpillar that inhabit North America, Mexico, and Eurasia. Many of them are often considered pests because they defoliate trees and shrubs, so eating them in the wild not only provides you with nutrition, but also reduces environmental degradation.

The eastern tent caterpillar is the larvae of the snout moth. It is believed to be toxic to horses but after cooking it no longer poses a threat to humans. Typically, eastern tent caterpillars are black and hairy with a white stripe and blue or red markings, though different colour variations exist. Many species of tent caterpillar are found across the U.S.

Tent caterpillars and other species of caterpillars can be eaten as part of a nutritious diet in the wild. They are easy to identify and collect because of the conspicuous silk tents that they build in the forks and crotches of trees. They are also active during the day and are often brightly colored, making them easy to spot. It's best to seek them out in late spring or summer, since the adult moth lays its eggs in early spring. They feed on deciduous trees and shrubs, especially apple, aspen, and wild cherry trees.

How To Eat:

People in northern Zambia, monitor caterpillar growth and adhere to strict harvesting schedules. Caterpillars are smoked and then stored for use in times of need.

There are many who eat deep-fried caterpillars in Mexico as a delicacy. Often, the caterpillars are seasoned with salt and chili and then served wrapped in a tortilla. Generally, caterpillars are high in protein, B vitamins, and iron, and have little fat. They can be dry roasted or fried in oil over a fire until they are crispy. You can also boil them though they won't be as crispy. For a 3.5 ounce serving, caterpillars provide 0.7 to 1.9 ounces of protein and 0.7 ounces of monounsaturated fat.

CHAPTER 6:

Mealworm

Insect Info:

Mealworms are the larvae of the mealworm beetle, a small blackish beetle that is found across the U.S. The mealworm has sometimes been confused with the tequila worm because of its close physical resemblance, though traditionally, the worm found in the bottom of a tequila bottle is the larva of the moth,*Hypoptaagavis*.

Mealworms can be farmed by feeding them on oats, wheat bran, grain, or other readily available foods such as potato or apple. Commercial farming of mealworms often incorporates the use of a juvenile hormone to preclude mealworms from maturing into beetles. This can lead to abnormal growth where larva can reach more than one-half an inch in length.

Mealworms are also used in pet foods for reptiles, fish, and birds, including bird feeders for wild birds. They are also widely available in shops as fishing bait and have gained increasing popularity in health food stores. However, they can be easily located in the wild. The best places to look are dark, cool, moist microhabitats, such as beneath rocks and fallen logs. Both the larva and the beetle are active at night and may be easier to find at this time, so don't forget to pack a flashlight. Because the larva feed on grain and seeds, they are often found in storerooms on farms where livestock feed is kept. They can even be found in flour supplies in kitchens.

There are many good reasons to eat mealworms. For one, they can be farmed sustainably, since a mealworm farm can be grown almost anywhere, from basements to closets. Also, mealworms are easy to collect because, unlike many other insects, they do not pose a threat when they are disturbed.

How To Eat:

Mealworms make an excellent food source because they are easy to collect and prepare, and are very nutritious. They can be baked or fried and are often sold as a healthy snack in specialist food stores. Roasting or frying them on low heat for around ten minutes flavouredwith garlic and salt can complement a larger meal such as a green salad.

The taste of the mealworm has been described as resembling almonds or other seeds and nuts. Mealworms can also be eaten raw, but cooking is highly recommended. Particularly if you worry you may struggle with the texture. Per 3.5 ounce serving, freeze-dried mealworms provide nearly five hundred calories and a staggering 1.6 ounces of protein, 1.3 ounces of fat and 0.24 ounces of carbohydrates making mealworms an important commodity when other foods are scarce.Please note that some people may be allergic to mealworms, particularly those allergic to shellfish so proceed with caution.

CHAPTER 7:

Honeybee Larvae

Insect Info:

Another kind of larvae that provides a good source of nutrition is that of the honeybee. Aside from the production of honey, sucrose-rich nectar, beeswax, and pollen, bees in their larval state provide an excellent food source in the wild.

Throughout North America, there are several species of honeybee, including the European honeybee and the more aggressive Africanized bee, which is a hybrid of an African subspecies and the European honeybee. Africanized bees are considerably larger than the European honeybee. Be wary when extracting larvae from Africanized beehives as they are much more likely to swarm.

Locating a beehive in the wild can be relatively easy and has been practiced by humans and animals for millennia. Most often, wild honeybee colonies are found in hollow trees.

Colonies can be found in the back country, as well in suburbs and cities. If you're living outdoors more permanently, and plan to establish your own apiary, nests are best sought out in the early spring months. During this time bees are still hungry after the long winter and are more susceptible to following scents. You can also locate colonies by tracking the route of a foraging worker bee. Once loaded with nectar, these bees fly back to the nest. However, this might involve a long wait in difficult terrain and a single honeybee might visit hundreds of flowers before returning home. A good way to resolve this is to attract bees with your own nectar source of equal portions of water and sugar, after which you can track a bee back to its hive.

How To Eat:

Bee larvae are eaten in many different cultures as a delicious treat. In China, bees and larvae are ground and ingested as a remedy for a sore throat. In Japan, bee larvae, or *Hachinoko*, are boiled before eating. Adult bees are also edible, providing they are cooked first to neutralize the poison in their stingers. Note that male bees do not have stingers.

Bee Larvae are found in the honeycomb cells of a colony and are whitish grubs about the size of a fingernail. Initially, larvae are fed on royal jelly, which is a secretion produced by worker bees that is sixty-seven percent water, 12.5 % crude protein, eleven percent simple sugars, as well as amino acids, fatty acids, B vitamins, and trace amounts of vitamin C. In addition to honey, royal jelly is farmed from hives by humans and significant deposits can be found in queen larvae cells of the hive, where it is stockpiled. Royal jelly is perishable and must be kept cool to preserve it for storage (honey or beeswax can be added to the mixture to prolong its shelf life.)

This diet of royal jelly makes the larvae sweet and rich. Typically, larvae provide over two hundred calories per 3.5 ounce serving, as well as over one-half ounce of protein, over one ounce of carbohydrate, one-quarter ounce of fat, B vitamins, and minerals, such as copper and manganese.

Larvae can be cooked or eaten raw. Being sweet in taste, they are especially good as a dessert. When fried in butter, the taste has been described as resembling bacon with a texture similar to mushroom.

CHAPTER 8:

Tibicen Cicada

Insect Info:

Cicadas are large winged insects that live underground for most of their lives. Some species emerge from their nests after lying dormant there for either thirteen or seventeen years, while other species emerge every year. They make a plentiful and nutritious food source that can be located and collected easily in the wild. Some species of cicadas can bite, although they very rarely do.

Cicadas are common across North America, particularly on the East Coast of the U.S. Native Americans have been known to eat cicadas and they are increasingly popular among hikers and outdoor enthusiasts. The most common cicada in the U.S belongs to the genus,*Tibicen*, which emerge every year and measure one to two inches in length. Often, they have green, brown, and black markings. A less common species is the *Magicicada*, which emerges every thirteen or seventeen years.

Cicadas emerge in late spring or early summer. Typically they live for two to six weeks and die off once they have laid their eggs. Since cicadas feed primarily on plant roots, it's worth avoiding land where you suspect the use of pesticides or herbicides as the ingestion of such things can be dangerous. It's best to look for cicadas as the sun is rising, since cicadas emerge from the ground during the night before shedding their nymph skin and climbing a tree or plant. Cicadas cannot fly until their wings and exoskeleton have hardened and often climb upwards to escape predators. Often, when searching for freshly emerged cicadas, known as teneral cicadas, you'll find discarded carapaces, or discarded skins at the base of a tree. Cicadas can easily be identified by their clear wings which resemble those of a dragonfly, their prominent eyes that are set wide apart, and their bulky bodies, which range in color from brown to grey to black. The earlier you arrive in the morning, the better your chances of collection. Cicadas can also be identified by the loud clicking sound, which male insects produce by the contraction of internal muscles, which is then amplified by the insect's largely hollow abdomen.

How To Eat:

It's best to eat cicadas as soon as possible after collection, since their carapaces harden quickly. Cicadas should be cooked before eating. A good method is to boil themas you would shrimp for a few minutes, though they can also be roasted or fried. They can also be roasted, dried, and stored for later use. Remove the wings and legs before eating to avoid a bitter and unpleasant crunch. Because cicadas feed mainly on juices from plants and trees, they are rich in protein and other nutrients. Cicadas are 46%-72% protein, are low in fat, and provide few carbohydrates. Cooked cicadas have been compared to shrimp because of their taste and general appearance.

CHAPTER 9:

European Earthworm

Insect Info:

Earthworms are tube-shaped segmented worms that provide perhaps the most plentiful and easily collected insect food source for those surviving in the wild. During the seventeenth century, the native earthworm of continental Europe migrated to North America where it is currently considered an invasive species, so all the better to collect and eat them.

Earthworms are used on a commercial scale in the U.S and elsewhere to create nutrient-rich compost for growing plants. They are also used to decompose food waste, and as fishing bait. They inhabit rich, dark soil and feed on live and dead organic matter, particularly leaf litter. There are more than 6,000 recognized species of earthworms throughout the world. Although only a small number of these are distributed across North America, they can be found in abundance in a range of different terrains.

Earthworms can be located simply by digging in fairly damp ground in fields, open meadow and woodlands. They can also be found above ground after heavy rain. Some reports have suggested that up to 1.75 million earthworms can be found per acre of land.

How To Eat:

Earthworms have been eaten by Native Americans, Aboriginal people in Australia, the Maoris of New Zealand and in parts of China. In New Zealand, they are a popular delicacy called,*Noke*.

Earthworms can be boiled, roasted, or fried. Boiling is the most popular method since the process effectively eliminates the mucus and any harmful bacteria. Boil continuously for ten minutes before eating. Earthworms can also be roasted and ground into powder for storage and later use. Earthworms are made up of as much as 82% protein, and many species contain the healthy Omega-3 fatty acids also found in oily fish. Because earthworms have an earthy flavour they are particularly good in curries with spices like cumin and turmeric. Placing earthworms in moist cornmeal or flour will effectively purge the worms of soil, making them much more palatable. Of course this depends on personal taste and the availability of supplies.

Note that many worms carry parasites and bacteria that may be harmful to humans. It is important to ensure that worms are cooked thoroughly before consuming.

CHAPTER 10:

Giant Redheaded Centipede

Insect Info:

Centipedes are arthropods similar to millipedes, though they have one pair of legs per body segment, whereas the millipede has two pairs of jointed legs per segment. Many species of millipedes are also edible, though both can be toxic. The giant redheaded centipede is a fast-moving and aggressive centipede, but catching one could provide you with a substantial nutritional snack since they are among the largest of the centipedes, measuring on average six and a half inches in length.

Note that some larger species of centipede, including the giant redheaded variety, can deliver a painful bite causing severe swelling, fever and weakness, though these bites are very rarely fatal. Smaller centipedes might also bite although they are unable to puncture human skin. Most centipedes move quickly due to their numerous legs and are therefore difficult to catch. Despite these factors, centipedes are often consumed by humans for their nutritional value which provides a significant source of important calories.

Giant redheaded centipedes are widely distributed in the southern states of the U.S., particularly in rocky woodland areas. In general, centipedes can be found in dark and moist microhabitats across many different habitat types, including savannahs, forests, agricultural land, and deserts. The best places to search and collect them include underneath stones, leaf litter, and in soil. They are mostly nocturnal creatures so searching in the early evening or early morning is a good idea.

How To Eat:

Centipedes are sold as street food and are used in traditional medicine in parts of China. In medicine, centipede extracts are used as a laxative and to dissipate toxins. In Thailand and Vietnam, giant centipedes are farmed, cooked, and eaten. They are even sold online as a whole or in powdered form. In Thailand and Vietnam, centipedes are roasted until crispy, and then seasoned with salt or dipped in sweet chili sauce.

Centipedes vary in size, though often measure four to eight inches in length and can range in color from yellow to reddish brown. As the name suggests, the giant redheaded centipede has a bright red head, as well as a long black body with yellow legs.

They can be grilled on wooden sticks until they are crispy, or they can be fried in oil. Because of its shell and legs, the centipede has a significant crunch to it, but if your options are limited, it could provide a valuable food source. Centipedes can also be boiled or dried and stored for later consumption, or ground into powder for use in herbal preparations. Centipedes have less protein than the grasshopper, termite, and June bug, though they do provide carbohydrates and are low in sodium and do not contain cholesterol. The taste has been described as bitter and salty. Note, please remember to remove the head and pincers before eating.

CONCLUSION

When searching for edible insects in the wild, remember that often, the flavour and texture of an insect can be determined by what the animal eats and the habitat in which it lives. Entomophagy also depends on the stage of growth of the insect in question. Larvae may be more palatable to eat than hard beetles with shells, wings, and legs, or centipedes with pincers. You should also take into consideration the method of collection needed for insects. For example, digging for irritable ants takes much more effort than herding grasshoppers into a tarp.

Aside from the ten insect types mentioned in this book, there are numerous other insects that can be eaten as part of a nutritious diet for both the casual camper and survivalists spending longer periods in the wild. Remember to be cautious and check that what you are eating is non-toxic and be sure to cook insects before eating.

Book 3

Survival Guide:

Hunting, Trapping, Fishing, and Outdoor Cooking

How to Survive by Using Primitive Hunting, Fishing, Trapping and Cooking Skills

TABLE OF CONTENTS

INTRODUCTION

This book was written for anyone who has an interest in hunting, trapping, fishing, and cooking small game animals. Here you will learn different methods for securing your own food in the wild. This book is ideal for both the diehard survivalists, and the average camper who wants to know how to catch, prepare, and cook their own food.

As you'll learn, all of the methods described in this book can be fruitful using natural materials alone, whether constructing traps or weapons.

CHAPTER 1:

Hunting, Fishing, and Trapping

Effective hunting, trapping, and fishing depend on careful observation and knowledge of the animals you intend to capture and the terrain they inhabit. Study the habits of the animal you are seeking. Discover where it sleeps, what it eats, and where it finds water. Often, identifying the signs animals leave behind will help you determine how best to capture them. Certain animals will be easier to identify than others. Foxes, for example, have a pungent scent and wild cats produce a strong-smelling urine.

Track the subtle signs that animals leave behind. Particularly focus on the trails between their watering holes and feeding grounds, looking for broken twigs and branches. Trails are clearest in wet ground, snow, and damp sand. When checking trails early in the morning, pay special attention to areas with disturbed dew or broken spider webs. Other signs include trampled leaves, droppings, gnawed bark, food or prey remains (which can be used for bait.)

The best time to hunt is at dawn and dusk when animals are most active, though most small mammals feed at night. When stalking prey on foot, proceed quietly, moving slowly and stopping regularly. Remember to keep your weight on your back feet, testing your next steps with your toes before transferring your entire body weight. Hunting against the wind reduces the chance that an animal will detect your scent first causing them to leave the area. If the animal you are hunting sees you, freeze. Often, the animal will simply be curious for a little while before looking away and continuing feeding. Don't give them a reason to run, but proceed with caution.

A wide variety of weapons can be used for hunting, including the bow and arrow, a blowgun with darts, the apache throwing star, a slingshot, and the split tip gig, some of which are described in the following chapters. For fishing, you can use a simple hand line or rod, as well as nightlines and basic traps.

There are numerous trapping methods for small mammals and birds, all of which dispatch prey by the following four methods: strangle, dangle, mangle and tangle (some combine these methods). Snare traps strangle prey. Spring traps employ sapling branches to dangle prey in the air. Deadfall traps mangle prey using a large weight. A the use of a net tangles prey.

CHAPTER 2:

Small Mammals – Snare Traps

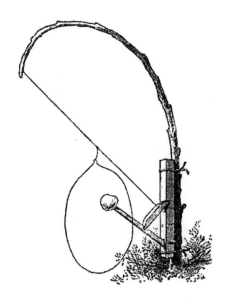

Prey and Trap Info:

Small prey are easier to trap than hunt. When planning a trap, the most important considerations are the bait you set your trap with and the site you choose for your trap. When setting any kind of trap for animals, it's crucial to be patient – animals will be wary at first – and it's equally important to check traps regularly. An unchecked trap may unnecessarily prolong an animal's pain and will increase the chance of their escape. Trapped animals may even bite off a limb to escape and you will also risk other predators coming along to take the prey for themselves.

A large range of small mammals can be caught using snares, including foxes, small wild cats, weasels, squirrels, opossums, raccoons, hares, and rabbits. Rabbits are perhaps the best option for any survivalist since they are abundant, widespread, and easy to catch. Rabbits live in burrows and use well-established runs, which is where snares can be set. Search for the small tough pellet droppings that are a strong indication of rabbits. Also look for nibbled bark at the base of tree trunks. Hares are more difficult prey to catch because they do not keep to the same runs and paths, making them much less common than rabbits.

It is important to note that you cannot survive by eating rabbits alone, no matter how many you eat. You will need important vitamins and minerals found in other sources of nutrition.

Other small mammals that can be caught easily include the cat-sized raccoon, which is found in plentiful across North America and is active by night. Alsoavailable in abundance are squirrels, which can be dispatched in the trees they inhabit using various long-range weapons (see chapter seven.)

Trapping Methods:

For the rabbit, the most effective trapping method is a simple wire or twine snare secured to a trunk or branch (as shown above.) When snaring small game in the wild, you must first determine the best place to set your snare by identifying a well defined run.

Remember that most small mammals feed at night, so setting your snares before dusk and checking at first light is the most productive method. Set traps along runs that pass under an obstruction and along natural bottlenecks where animals are likely to venture. Do not place a trap near a burrow; it will soon notice the disturbance.

When setting any trap, avoid disturbing the surrounding environment. This includes not treading on trails or leaving objects or other signs behind that will alert the prey to your presence. It's also important to acknowledge the environment where traps are set. For example, do not construct an evergreen trap in deciduous woodland. Also, be sure not to handle the traps - hide your scent by wearing gloves. You can mask human scent by exposing wood to campfire smoke.

There are numerous other types of snare traps, including stepped-bait snares, toggle snares, and baited-hole-noose snares, all of which can be used for small mammals. To snare tree squirrels, use a loop snare attached to a pole, which you then lean against a tree trunk. For the bait, use split fruit or a bird egg.

If you're living in the wild for an extended period of time, collect and reset your traps often, repairing them when necessary and removing any that are repeatedly fruitless. If the bait is missing from your trap, your trigger mechanism may be too tight or the bait may have been insecurely fixed. For fast-moving animals like rabbits, you can also try the Apache throwing star, which is a throwing weapon comprised of two sticks lashed together to make four sharp points.

CHAPTER 3:

Small Mammals – Spring Traps

Prey and Trap Info:

Spring traps use the tension of saplings and nooses to strangle and then dangle prey high above ground, out of the way of other animals. Like basic snares, they are especially effective for catching rabbits, foxes, and other small mammals. It's a good idea to set your spring snares on trails where there's a natural bottleneck caused by an obstruction. Spring traps may be better suited for long-term survivors who have set multiple, traps since prey is safer for longer periods when suspended above the ground. Spring traps are also a good idea for fast-reacting animals like felines that might wriggle free of snares and may leap clear of deadfall traps.

Trapping Methods:

A simple spring trap can be made by cutting a notch in a trigger bar (a) to fit a notch in an upright (b) as shown. Then, secure the upright into the ground using a stone or other heavy tool.

Next, attach a snare to the trigger bar and attach a cord or strong string to a sapling under tension as pictured. When the bar disengages, the snared game is lifted into the air. The larger the sapling, the higher the game will dangle, which will keep your catch out of the reach of other animals.

A spring tension snare can also be used for small animals. This is a slightly more advanced version of the simple snare trap since it uses what's called a keeper stick to keep the noose suspended above ground. Other spring traps for small prey include the trapeze spring trap and the roller spring trap. The trapeze trap uses two snares to catch game where two trials run parallel to each other. This will double your success rate, allowing you to snare two animals at once. You can of course attach as many snares as you like. The roller spring trap uses a rounded grip hold for a notch – rather than the upright notch shown above – and works especially well for rabbits and foxes.

Other spring traps include the baited spring leg snare, platform spring traps, and stepped bait release snares, but these are better for larger prey such as deer, wild pigs, and large carnivores.

CHAPTER 4:

Small Mammals – Deadfall Traps

Prey and Trap Info:

Typically, deadfall traps work by luring animals in to take the bait. Once the bait is disturbed, the trap's mechanism is activated and a heavy weight falls on the prey. Some deadfall traps use a trip wire to activate the mechanism. You should site a deadfall trap along a rabbit run or other animal trail for maximum results.

It is important to note that large deadfall traps can be dangerous to humans as well, so tread cautiously. By design, deadfall traps are easily triggered and can be set off accidentally. When setting traps, ensure that other people in the area are aware of trap sites. Deadfall traps should be set by more than one person and the trigger mechanism should be placed on the side of the trail, away from the dropping weight. Because of the effort involved, the deadfall trap is best used for large prey, though smaller traps can be used with great effect on small to medium-sized mammals as well.

Trapping Methods:

Setting the trigger mechanism can be difficult and you are unlikely to get it right the first time. The toggle trip-release trap incorporates a toggle-release snare with a suspended dropping weight made of heavy logs (as shown.)

The trap uses a trip release line that runs just above the ground and beneath the suspended logs. The idea is for the animal to activate the trip line causing the excess weight to fall and trap the animal.

Another deadfall trap is the balance log trap. A sharpened fork stick holds the bait, which is attached to a forked branch that holds a row of angled logs that will fall on the animal once the bait is disturbed. Large stones can be gathered to use instead of logs. Plastic or wooden containers can also be used if you want to trap your prey alive. Deadfall traps that incorporate spears can be incredibly dangerous to humans. They use the same mechanism as deadfalls but with rocks and sharpened sticks to inflict a stabbing blow to prey as the mechanism is activated and the weight falls.

CHAPTER 5:

Fish and Crustaceans – Angling, Night Lines, Traps, and Nets

Prey and Fishing Info:

Fish and crustaceans are a plentiful and nutritious food source. They can be found in all bodies of water and offer high amounts of protein, vitamins, and fats. A successful fishing haul will depend on climate and temperature. If it's hot and water levels are low, fish will retreat to deeper waters. In cold weather, fish seek out shallow water to warm themselves. Typically, fish shelter under banks and rocks whatever the weather might be. During flooding, fish move to slacker water, such as the outside of a bend or in smaller tributaries. If a storm looms on the horizon,you should do your fishing before it breaks becauseyouwill yield poor results following a heavy rain.

It is best to fish during feeding times as the fish are much more active. Often, fish can be seen jumping out of the water to feed on insects, or when clear rings ripple across the water's surface. If you see lots of smaller fish moving erratically, it's likely a larger predatory fish is in pursuit.

Fishing Methods:

A variety of techniques can be used to catch fish and other marine animals. All fish can be attracted and caught with the appropriate bait. Angling, which is any method of fishing involving a hook, can be used to catch fish if you have plenty of time and enjoy the activity. If you have read our other book, *How To Create Basic Weapons For Hunting, Fishing, And Self Defense*, you'll know how easy it is to construct a bamboo fishing rod for catching small to medium-sized fish. Because wooden rods are lightweight, it is ideal for fly-fishing in rivers and streams.

Fishing hooks can be made from numerous materials, including pins, thorns, nails, bone, and wood. Of course, rods aren't a necessity for angling, since handlines can be used for smaller fish and crabs. A whole range of floats and weights, spinners, and artificial bait can be used to increase your success while angling.

Note that fish are more likely to take bait that is native to their habitat. This could include overhanging berries and insects in the vicinity. After your first catch, inspect the stomach contents of the fish to determine possibilities for future bait.

There are various other fishing methods, many of which are considered more effective, especially if other food sources are scarce. These methods include a simple fishing net attached to a long stave, gill nets, nightlines, and traps.

Nets can be constructed easily with fishing line, twine, or nylon. The gill net yields excellent results and is much less time-consuming than angling. When using a net, you should set floats along the top, and weight the bottom before stretching it across a river. A gill net will soon empty a stretch of water so do not leave unattended for too long. If you are fishing on your own, the net could easily become too heavy for you to retrieve.

To construct a night line, all you will need is: live bait (worms or crickets are best,) a fishing line, cord, or other material, some hooks, a piece of wood, and a large stone. Attach baited hooks at regular intervals along the line. Weight one end of the line with the stone and lower the line into a body of water from the bank at a forty-five degree angle. Anchor the other end securely on the bank by driving a piece of wood into the ground and fastening the line around the stake. Leave the line out overnight and check just before dawn. Lines can also be left out during the day, providing you replenish your bait often since live bait will attract more attention.

Various traps can be built for catching fish. One of the simplest traps can be made from a plastic bottle. Cut the top off the bottle just below the neck and invert the neck inside the bottle. Place bait inside the bottle and secure between some rocks on the bed of a stream or river. Once fish have been lured through the neck, they cannot swim out. Make sure you place the neck opening so that the current flows toward the bottle opening. Other more elaborate traps that work on the same principle can be made from logs or woven twigs. A baited, torpedo-shaped trap can be used to lure crayfish and lobster.

Whatever your technique, remember that fish can see out the water due to refraction. It's best to sit or kneel at the river's edge so as not to be seen, but also choose your seat so that your shadow is cast onto land and not over thethe water where you fish.

CHAPTER 6:

Birds and Fowl – Traps and Nets

Prey and Trap Info:

All birds and fowl are edible, though they vary in taste and toughness. Game birds, such as pheasant, partridge, and woodcock make an excellent meal but they are well camouflaged and innocuous in their environment. The meat of birds of prey is much tougher than other birds and must be boiled thoroughly.

When seeking out birds, large amounts of droppings indicate a nesting site. In autumn, birds molt and are unable to fly long distances, making them much easier to catch. Ducks, geese, and game birds are especially easy to hunt during this time.

Locating the nests of ground birds is an easy way to secure eggs and birds. Approach nests with caution – crawling is better than walking. When stalking waterfowl, the best tactic is to get into the water and camouflage your head using reeds or other vegetation. Large birds such as geese will attack you when they feel threatened, whether protecting their young or not. Be sure to carry a club or similar blunt weapon to protect yourself. Larger birds like ostriches should be avoided since they can deliver a powerful kick. When looking for birds in snow or desert regions, tracks can be followed to clover where birds will often take cover. Note, the alarm calls of birds often indicate the presence of larger, more dangerous animals.

Trapping Methods

The best methods for capturing birds that take bait (mostly small birds) are cage traps, deadfalls, and spring snares. For roosting birds, attach nooses to branches close to nests. In woodlands, place traps in clearings or next to riverbanks. You can make a crude dummy owl out of wood and feathers to lure small birds. For waterfowl, a line of snares can be suspended slightly above a stream where there are reeds and rushes.

Nets are often the fastest and most effective way to catch birds since several can be caught in one net. Once prey is tangled in the net, deliver a blow to the head with a club or blunt weapon. Stretch a fine net between trees where birds roost. You can also construct a net by criss-crossing twine between trees. Site your nets along a bird's flight path. Some birds can be approached and a weighted, or purse net, can be thrown over them. This is especially effective for flightless birds but be cautious around larger birds, which can easily become aggressive. An array of weapons can be used to capture birds, most of which are described in the following chapter.

CHAPTER 7:

Tree-Dwelling Animals – Weapons

Prey and Weapon Info:

A variety of improvised long-range weapons can be used to kill nesting birds, owls, and tree-dwelling animals, such as squirrels, pine martens, lemurs and small monkeys, as well as some species of snakes and lizards. The best way to capture these animals is to use long-range propulsion weapons from the ground, rather than setting traps and pursuing these animals up close. Be wary of nesting birds, which can be especially dangerous when protecting their young. What's more, trees often harbor unseen threats, including biting insects and dead branches, which can contribute to unnecessary falls.

Typically, birds build nests in the canopy (the very top of the tree) and often at the top of the tallest trees. Owls may occupy lower branches, but are mostly nocturnal, making them difficult targets. Squirrels are perhaps the most abundant tree-dwelling creatures and are also the easiest to catch. Other tree-dwelling mammals are shy and easily camouflaged in foliage. Large lizards and snakes are rarely seen occupying trees, though when they do appear, they often sun themselves on branches and trunks early in the mornings.

Hunting Methods:

The bow and arrow is probably the best weapon for capturing birds and tree-dwelling mammals since it is easy to make and takes only a short time to become proficient. When practicing your firing technique, fit the arrow into the bowstring, raise the centre of the bow to eye-level, and then hold the bow just below the arrow, straightening your arm while keeping your bow arm locked. Then draw the string back smoothly across the front of your body with the arrow at eye-level and in line with your target. Sight your target along the length of the arrow and once satisfied with your aim, release the string. Watch out for arrow burns when firing. Protect your cheek with a piece of cloth and wear a leather mitten to protect your straightened hand and wrist.

You can also use a blowgun or a slingshot, though they will be less effective against mammals larger than an owl and are not as accurate as the bow and arrow. Both the blowgun and the slingshot are a good choice for nesters and large birds. When using a slingshot, load with several pebbles or stones at once to maximize your chance of success. Once hit, approach the animal quickly with a club or other blunt weapon to ensure that it's dead. Blowgun darts are best used with poison. For detailed description on how to construct these weapons see our e-book, *How To Create Basic Weapons For Hunting, Fishing, And Self Defense.*

CHAPTER 8:

Amphibians, Reptiles, and Rodents – Split Tip Gig

Prey and Weapon Info:

The split tip gig is the best weapon for catching amphibians, reptiles, rodents and other small mammals that are too small to snare. Amphibians include frogs, toads, and newts. Reptiles include lizards and snakes. Rodents include rats, mice, and guinea pigs. Note that some frogs have poisonous skin, though all are edible. Toads have warty skin and may be found far from water. Most have toxic skin, which should not be eaten. Many lizards and snakes are timid, can move quickly, and may inflict painful and sometimes poisonous bites. Rats and other rodents often carry disease and may inflict bites when provoked.

Despite these concerns, all of these animals can be caught easily and make good eating when prepared and cooked properly. Most, if not all animals in these categories are most active at night, and many live close to water.

Hunting Methods:

In our e-book, *How To Create Basic Weapons For Hunting, Fishing, And Self Defense*, we described how to make a split tip gig from natural materials. This weapon is excellent for opportunistic hunting for the animals mentioned above. Essentially, the split tip is a long pole with four sharp tines at the end that can be used for jabbing and stabbing animals on the ground.

To aid your hunt, before stabbing frogs and other amphibians, shine a bright light in their eyes to dazzle them, causing them to freeze. The split tip gig is also an excellent weapon for catching snakes, though be wary of large or poisonous snakes. Ensure that snakes are dead before removing the gig since some snakes feign death very convincingly. The split tip gig can also be used to catch fish and other marine animals.

CHAPTER 9:

Handling the Kill

After the Kill:

Before approaching, check that your prey is dead. Many small animals can deliver painful bites, especially when injured. Tie your knife to a long stick and stab the animal in the neck or inflict a blow to the head with a club or blunt weapon. For birds, stretch the neck and slit the throat. Your goal should always be to do this as humanely as possible.

Preparing the Kill:

When using traps, butcher the animal on the trap line. This may attract other animals for future kills and will avoid flies and scavengers at your camp. Also, entrails can be used to bait traps. If you have more prey than you can carry back to your camp, hide surplus food for later collection. Dead prey can be suspended from a tree branch, providing it's out of reach from tree-dwellers. However, if vultures are present, your cache will be impossible to protect.

Before taking your prey back to camp, check the animal for signs of disease. All animals have lymph glands in their cheeks. If these are large and discoloured, or if the animal's head is distorted or disfigured, handle prey with care by covering any cuts or sores you may have on your skin. Diseased animals should be discarded, or if food is especially scarce, they should be boiled thoroughly before eating. Discard all spoiled fish and marine animals.

Waste nothing when preparing the kill for eating. All parts of an animal that cannot be eaten can be used as bait, while bones and skins can often be fashioned into tools, utensils, and clothing.

Bleeding and Skinning:

Most small mammals require bleeding. Hang the animal vertically and make an incision on a major artery. For rabbits, you can sever the Achilles tendon just beneath the hock on the hind leg. Allow the blood to drain into a receptacle. Skin small mammals and rodents while the flesh is still warm. Remove scent glands (often behind the knees on the hind legs, or as in the case of felines, on either side of the anus.) Remove testicles on male animals. To skin, first make an incision over the stomach while taking care not to pierce internal organs. Insert thumbs and pull outwards. Once you have freed the legs, twist off the head. If you don't have a knife you can use the sharp edge of the animal's leg bone.

Hang birds head down to bleed. Carnivorous birds harbor parasites and must be handled as little as possible. Pluck feathers while the body is still warm. Use hot water to loosen feathers (except for waterfowl). Birds do not require skinning before eating.

For reptiles, discard internal organs and cook with the skin on. Remove the head behind any poison glands, especially for snakes. Some frogs have poisonous skin,which should be removed before cooking.

Gutting:

When gutting small mammals and rodents, be very careful not to rupture the innards, which will spoil the meat. This is especially important when removing the gut and offal. Remove heart, lungs, liver, kidneys, and pancreas, and put to one side for cooking. You should also remove the windpipe and check that the anus is clear. Discard the liver or lungs if they are mottled or spotted white or black.

Jointing

Cuts vary according to the animal. Typically, the best cuts are the legs and the breast. All of the offal should be eaten as soon as possible, or it can be used to bait traps. Tail, feet, head, and bones can be boiled to add flavourto stews and soups.

Fish and Crustaceans

Fish undertwo inches in length can be cooked and eaten whole. Larger fish must be gutted. After catching fish, cut its throat to bleed and remove the gills. To gut, cut from the anal orifice to the throat and remove the offal. Fish scales can be removed if you like, though it isn't necessary.

Eat crustaceans as soon as possible. Note that crabs have poisonous parts that must be removed before eating. Twist off legs and claws and place the crab on its back. The place your thumbs underneath the flap at the tail and push up. Pull the flap up and away from the crab's body before lifting off – this prevents tainting the flesh. Then remove the mouth and stomach by pushing down on the mouth with your thumbs and lifting both of them away in one piece. Finally, remove the lungs, which are also poisonous.

CHAPTER 10:

Cooking – Fires, Methods, and Tips

Cooking makes food more appetizing and easy to digest and is advised for all small prey, including fish and crustaceans. Cooking also destroys bacteria and parasites and neutralizes poisons. However, cooking reduces the nutritional value of food, so refrain from cooking for longer than necessary.

Fires

There are numerous ways to cook in the wild, often depending on what you are cooking and how much effort you want to expend. The trench fire is especially good for roasting and grilling meat. First, dig a trench measuring 12 x 36 inches with a depth of one foot. Line the bottom of the trench with rocks and construct a fire on top. Even once the embers have died down the rocks will retain enough heat for cooking.

To boil food, make a hobo stove using an oil drum, paint cans, or food cans for example. First, make holes in the bottom of the drum and around the bottom edge. Cut out a panel on one side, allowing you to stoke the fire. Set the drum on a ring of stones to allow ventilation underneath. A pot or pan can then be placed on top of the drum.

Methods

When cooking on open fire, boil water when the flames are high and use the embers to grill and roast. It's a good idea to have water boiling constantly – unless you are in short supply of water – for drinking and for sterilizing wounds. Rather than balancing a boiling pot on the fire, support it using rocks or suspend above two upright sticks outside of the fire with a supporting beam of green wood that has been soaked in water to prevent it from burning.

There are numerous methods for cooking small prey and often this depends on the animal. The most common methods include boiling, steaming, roasting, grilling, baking, and frying, all of which can be used with ease on an open fire.

Tips

Meat from small game can be cooked in joints or cut into cubes before cooking. Check that offal is firm, odourless, and free from lumps or discoloration before cooking. Offal is best roasted or fried. Drained blood can also be used to thicken stews and soups.

Skewer reptiles and amphibians on sharp sticks of green wood before roasting over hot embers. When the skin starts to split, remove and boil. Cook rodents thoroughly by boiling, grilling, or skewering on a stick.

For birds, boil all carrion as well as older and carnivorous birds. Young birds can be roasted on a spit or in an earthen or metal oven. Eggs can be boiled, or roasted on hot embers after piercing them at one end. Some eggs may contain embryos, which can be removed and roasted.

Fish can be stewed or wrapped in non-toxic leaves and placed on hot embers. Boil crustaceans for twenty minutes.

CONCLUSION

Aside from the methods mentioned in this book, there are numerous other ways to catch and kill small game for food while in the wild. In many cases, your methods will be determined by your available resources, whether natural or otherwise, and alsoby your environment and the animals that inhabit that area.

Whenever in the wild, it's important to respect habitats and endangered species. You should avoid hunting and killing rare animal species, such as birds of prey and larger mammals such as elk. This book is best used to hunt for small, abundant and widespread prey like rabbits, squirrels, and game birds.

PREVIEW OF 'PREPPING: BOOBY TRAPS'

Booby Traps:

Typically, a booby trap is a triggered device that lures an intruder with the intention of killing, disengaging, or surprising him or her. In this e-book, we describe booby traps and techniques that are intended to protect you and your home from a direct threat to your safety. In an extreme survival situation, a threat is considered anyone attempting to enter your property without permission and with criminal intent. This includes thieves, looters, or gangs in the wake of natural or social upheaval.

Natural, social, and economic disasters can lead to a scenario where your home, family, food and weapons can come under threat. If you predict a looming disaster, monitor weather forecasts for news about severe weather conditions. Natural disasters include droughts, forest fires, flooding, tsunamis, avalanches, hurricanes, tornados, earthquakes, volcanoes, and mud flows. Arguably, social and economic disasters are much harder to predict, though many news sources can be monitored if rioting or other extreme behaviour begin to spread in your area.

The booby trap is an excellent method for deterring these threats because it avoids direct violence. However, before implementing traps, consider how secure your home is and whether or not traps are likely to provoke future, more intent intruders. Also consider whether or not they are necessary at all. We recommend that unless you are in immediate danger, it's best to employ non-lethal methods.

BONUS!

Be the first to get survival guides, gear, and books before everyone else at half price! Enter your email address at **SurvivalHax.com/join** to be a part of the fastest growing community of campers, hikers and preppers.

Sign ups today receive **10% off** the Survival Water Filter on Amazon.